LET'S
see

# Farm Crops

by Jennifer Blizin Gillis

Content Adviser: Susan Thompson, Agriculture Communications,
College of Agriculture, Iowa State University

Reading Adviser: Rosemary Palmer, Ph.D.,
Department of Literacy, College of Education,
Boise State University

Let's See Library
Compass Point Books
Minneapolis, Minnesota

Compass Point Books
3109 West 50th Street, #115
Minneapolis, MN 55410

Visit Compass Point Books on the Internet at *www.compasspointbooks.com*
or e-mail your request to *custserv@compasspointbooks.com*

On the cover: Rows of corn grow in a field in the Midwest.

Photographs ©: Brand X Pictures, cover; Corbis, 4, 12, 16; Photodisc, 6, 8, 18; U.S. Department of
Agriculture/Bill Tarpenning, 10; Inga Spence/Visuals Unlimited, 14; U.S. Department of Agriculture, 20.

Creative Director: Terri Foley
Managing Editor: Catherine Neitge
Editors: Brenda Haugen and Christianne Jones
Photo Researcher: Marcie C. Spence
Designers: Melissa Kes and Jaime Martens
Educational Consultant: Diane Smolinski

**Library of Congress Cataloging-in-Publication Data**
Gillis, Jennifer Blizin, 1950-
   Farm crops / by Jennifer B. Gillis.
       p. cm. — (Let's see)
Includes index.
ISBN 0-7565-0669-7 (hardcover)
   1. Food crops—Juvenile literature. I. Title. II. Series.
SB175.G55 2004
630—dc22                                    2003028294

# Table of Contents

*NOTE: In this book, words that are defined in the glossary are in* **bold** *the first time they appear in the text.*

4

# What Are Crops?

Some farmers grow fields of golden wheat. Others grow bright yellow sunflowers. Some fields are filled with tall cornstalks. These are just a few of the crops farmers grow.

Crops often are used as food for people or animals. Crops also can be used to make **products** people use, such as ink, cloth, or **fuel.**

All around the world, farmers grow crops. Some crops, such as wheat and corn, can grow almost anywhere. Other crops, such as oranges and cotton, only grow in places where the weather stays warm most of the year. That is because these crops take longer to grow.

◄ *Wheat grows in a field.*

# How Do Crops Start?

All plants grow from seeds. Most crops come from new seeds each season. Sometimes farmers save seeds from healthy plants and plant them the next year. Usually they buy new seeds each year to make sure the plants they grow will be good ones.

Fruit trees or bushes that grow from seeds live for a long time. They bear fruit for many years. Farmers may plant some seeds to add new trees and bushes each year. This way, there will always be young trees to take the places of older trees that die.

◄ *Wheat seeds*

# Why Is Soil Important?

Most crops grow in **soil.** Good soil helps make healthy crops. The crops take nutrients from the soil as they grow. Nutrients are the materials a living thing needs to live and grow.

When it is time for farmers to plant crops, they get the soil ready. Sometimes the soil is heavy and covered with old plant parts from the last year. Farmers may use **plows** or **discs** on the fields to break up the soil and chop up tough plant parts.

Sometimes farmers put **fertilizer** into the soil. Fertilizer helps plants grow strong and healthy. After fertilizer is used, farmers can plant seeds for a new crop.

◀ *A farmer tills a field to get it ready to plant crops.*

# What Are Grain Crops?

Crops farmers grow to make cereal, bread, or rice products are called grain crops. People eat the grains, which are the plant's seeds. Grains such as wheat and oats are in the head of the plant at the top of the stalk. Corn **kernels** grow on cobs called ears. It takes many plants to make enough grain for cereal or flour, so farmers plant big fields of crops.

Corn is a grain crop with many uses. People and animals eat corn. It also is used in fuel for cars and trucks. Ethanol is a corn product that can be mixed with gasoline.

◄ *A farmer in Mississippi looks at his corn.*

# How Do Farmers Grow Fruits and Vegetables?

On small farms, farmers may grow different kinds of fruits and vegetables. On larger farms, there may be just one kind of crop, such as tomatoes or potatoes. Some fruits and vegetables need lots of room to grow. Pumpkins and melons grow on long vines that spread out across the ground. Farmers must plant them in large fields.

On big farms, machines plant vegetable and fruit seeds. The machines can plant many rows of seeds at once. Workers check the plants as they grow to make sure they are healthy.

◄ Pumpkins grow on vines in a pumpkin patch.

# How Do Farmers Grow Fruits and Nuts on Trees?

Many fruits and nuts grow on large trees. A field of these trees can be called an orchard or a grove.

The trees flower each year. When the flowers die, fruit or nuts grow in their place. The fruit or nuts stay on the tree for several months to become **ripe.** When they are ripe, they can be picked.

Farmers sometimes join two different kinds of fruit or nut trees together. This is called **grafting.** They do this to create trees that will bear more fruit or be healthier. Farmers have made apple trees that grow red and green apples at the same time!

◄ *A worker grafts a part of a Fuji apple tree to a Granny Smith apple tree.*

# What Are Some Other Crops?

Soybeans are a crop that people and animals eat. They also can be used to make ink, fuel, and glue. Soybeans grow in pods that look like the green beans people eat.

Sunflowers also are a useful crop. The head of each sunflower plant holds hundreds of seeds. Sunflower seeds can be pressed to make oil. People also eat dried sunflower seeds. Many animals eat dried sunflower seeds, too. Pet stores sell treats for animals that include sunflower seeds.

Some farmers grow cotton. The plants grow fluffy, white cotton **bolls.** The bolls are **processed** and woven into cloth for clothes and towels.

◄ *Sunflowers grow in a field.*

# How Do Farmers Care for Crops?

All crops need good soil, water, and sunshine to grow. If there is not enough rain, some farmers water the crops. On some farms, huge sprinklers roll through fields to spray water. Other farmers bring water to their fields through pipes called **irrigation** systems.

Farmers must protect crops from insects that might eat them. They also must keep weeds from growing too close to the crops and stealing nutrients. Farmers sometimes spray crops with chemicals that kill insects and weeds. They also use machines called cultivators to pull out weeds.

◀ *Sprinklers water crops in a field.*

# How Do Farmers Pick Crops?

Some crops are **harvested** by hand. Farmers hire extra workers to help them. The workers walk through the fields and pick each fruit or vegetable from the trees, bushes, or vines. The workers put the fruits or vegetables into big boxes, bags, or baskets.

Machines harvest many crops. Big machines called combines cut down huge fields of crops such as wheat or corn. Other machines can dig up potatoes or even pick tomatoes. The machines save the parts of the plants that farmers sell and dump other parts of the plants back onto the fields. The parts dumped on the ground make more nutrients in the soil.

◄ *Workers harvest yellow squash.*

# Glossary

**bolls**—pods on a cotton plant that hold the seeds

**discs**—farm machines with very sharp, round metal pieces that can chop up tough parts of old plants

**fertilizer**—a material that enriches the soil

**fuel**—something that makes heat or energy, such as oil

**grafting**—planting part of one plant onto another so they grow as one

**harvested**—picked or gathered

**irrigation**—a way of bringing water to crops

**kernels**—whole seeds from plants such as corn

**plows**—machines with metal blades that break up and turn over dirt

**processed**—prepared or changed by a series of steps

**products**—things that are made or manufactured

**ripe**—ready to be picked or eaten

**soil**—a mixture of broken-up rock and bits of dead plants and animals

# Did You Know?

• Grapes grow on vines in fields called vineyards. The grapes people eat are called table grapes. Dried grapes are called raisins. It takes 4½ pounds (2 kilograms) of grapes to make 1 pound (½ kilogram) of raisins.

• Potatoes are sold fresh and processed by freezing, canning, and cooking. They are so popular that each person in the United States eats about 125 pounds (56 kilograms) of potatoes each year! Idaho grows more potatoes than any other state in the country.

# Want to Know More?

## In the Library

Hall, Margaret. *Corn.* Chicago: Heinemann
   Library, 2002.

Shepard, Daniel. *All Kinds of Farms.*
   Bloomington, Minn.: Yellow Umbrella
   Books, 2004.

Stone, Lynn M. *Farm Crops.* Vero Beach,
   Fla.: Rourke Publishing, 2001.

Wolfman, Judy. *Life on a Crop Farm.*
   Minneapolis: Lerner, 2001.

## On the Web

For more information on *farm crops,*
use FactHound to track down Web sites
related to this book.

1. Go to *www.facthound.com*
2. Type in a search word related to this
   book or this book ID: 0756506697.
3. Click on the *Fetch It* button.

Your trusty FactHound will fetch the best
Web sites for you!

## On the Road

Canton Learning Farm
2043 State Highway 68
Canton, NY 13617
315/379-0607
To visit a teaching and research
demonstration farm

Autumn Acres
1096 Baier Road
Crossville, TN 38555
931/707-0103
To visit a corn maze
and pumpkin patch

# Index

## About the Author

Jennifer Blizin Gillis writes poetry and nonfiction books for children. She lives on a former dairy farm in Pittsboro, North Carolina, with her husband, a dog, and a cat. She is more of a gardener than a farmer, but has lived on farms and in farming communities.